Happy Mother's Day!
MOMMY!
From,

This is your day Mommy!

I love you mommy!

Mommy,
You create magic!

Mommy,
You are super!

Mommy,
Thank you for all you do!

You've got this Mommy!

You've got this Mommy!

To the World's Best MOMMY!

Mommy,
A beautiful flower just for you!

Every day is special with a MOMMY like you!

Have some fun today!

Hugs and kisses to you!

You are my hero!

You are my hero!

BEST
MOM
EVER

You are always in my heart!

You are always in my heart!

Happy Mother's Day Mommy!
Coloring Card